Economists agree: The single ... job growth in the United Sta... intelligence.

America is finally approaching full employment. But a chorus of experts claims that this happy situation will be short-lived. Their warning is not the usual one about unemployment rising again when the next recession hits. Instead, the proposition is more ominous: that technology is finally able to replace people in most jobs.

The idea that we face a future without work for a widening swath of the citizenry is animated by the astonishing power of algorithms, artificial intelligence (AI) and automation, especially in the form of robots. At last count, more than a dozen expert studies, each sparking a flurry of media attention, have offered essentially the same conclusion: that the amazing power of emerging technologies today really *is* different from anything we've seen before; that is, the coming advances in labor productivity will be so effective as to eliminate most labor.

It has become fashionable in Silicon Valley to believe that, in the near future, those with jobs will comprise a minority of "knowledge workers." This school of thought proposes carving off some of the wealth surplus generated by our digital overlords to support a Universal Basic Income for the inessential and unemployable, who can then engage in whatever pastime their heart desires, except working for a wage.

It is true that something unprecedented *is* happening. America is in the early days of a structural revolution in technology, one that will culminate in an entirely new kind of infrastructure, one that democratizes AI in all its forms. This essay focuses on the factual and deductive problems with the associated end-of-jobs claim. In it, we explore what recent history and the data reveal about the nature of AI and robots, and how those technologies might impact work in the 21st century.

But before mapping out the technological shift now underway and its future implications, let's look for context at previous revolutions in labor productivity.

Grand transitions in productivity are episodic and powerful

One of humanity's oldest pursuits is inventing machines that reduce the labor-hours needed to perform tasks. History offers hundreds of examples. Each invention seemed amazing in its era. To note a handful of examples, in modern times, we have seen the arrival of the automatic washing machine in the 1920s; the programmable logic controller

History demonstrates that, when it comes to major technological dislocations, most forecasts get both the "what" and the "when" wrong.

(PLC), which enabled the first era of manufacturing automation in 1968; the word processor in 1976; and the first computer spreadsheet in 1979.

As with the "typing pools," rows of accountants "ciphering," rooms full of draftsmen with sharp pencils, or other common workplace sights from bygone eras, it is easy to predict which groups will lose jobs from gains in labor productivity. It is far harder, on the other hand, to predict the kinds of *new* jobs and how many will appear. It's easy to see how an economy expanding due to accelerated productivity leads to added wealth, which, in turn, leads to more demand for existing products and services, all of which entail labor. But it is more challenging to predict the specifics of how new technologies invariably lead to unanticipated businesses producing new kinds of products and services, all employing people in entirely novel ways.

One of the most powerful advances in the history of labor productivity was the arrival in 1913 of a practical automobile. The very word "automobile" was coined to describe the automation of mobility, a long-time goal of humanity. The transition from grain-fed horses to petroleum-fueled automobiles took place with astonishing velocity precisely because the productivity benefits were so profound. (See Figure 1.) Along the way, as every schoolchild learns, the automobile totally upended the character and locus of every kind of employment associated with centuries of transportation services. Gone forever were all the jobs and millions of acres of land devoted to the feeding, care and use of horses.

The 1956 invention of the shipping container – an idea patented by U.S. trucking-company owner Malcolm McLean – also radically increased labor productivity. Containerization

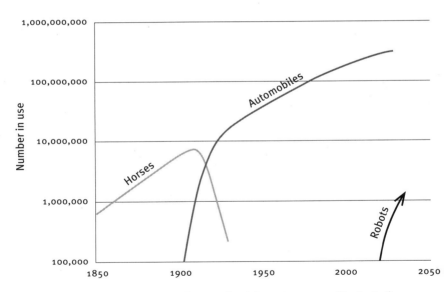

Figure 1   Grand Transitions in Labor Productivity, 1850–2050 (Projected)
Source: Adapted from Nakicenovic, Nebojsa

led to a 2,000% gain in shipping productivity in just five years and the end of centuries of rising employment for longshoremen (and, historically, they were all men). That gain in productivity rivaled that which took place in the previous century with the switch from sail to steam power: both radically lowered shipping costs, and both propelled world trade, prosperity and, derivatively, employment.

Containerization is also a clear example of how a new mode of business is made possible by building on a machine-based infrastructure invented and deployed by others: containerization could not have been effected prior to the availability of the precision powered cranes and gantries. That model matches exactly what Sears and Roebuck did in 1892, using the existing railroad infrastructure to launch their revolutionary retail empire, and what Amazon did a century later, using the existing Internet infrastructure to do the same.

One could wax lyrical about the pursuit of productivity. After all, the single most precious resource in the universe is the corporeal time we humans have. Maybe, someday, genetic engineers will find magic to change that. But it remains the case that every human being is born with a "bank" account with a maximum balance of about one million living hours. As with money, a million sounds like a lot – until you start consuming it.

***Technology is the only leverage we've ever
had to "buy" time***

Using technology to reduce or amplify human labor is
more than metaphysical, though. Productivity is central to
economic progress. As economic historian Joel Mokyr has
pointed out, technological innovation gives society the
closest thing there is to a "free lunch." From the dawn of
the industrial revolution, it has enabled the near-magical
increase in the availability of *everything*, from food and
fuel to every imaginable service. There is an enormous
body of scholarship devoted to the study of how productivity increases both wealth and employment. Providing a
coherent theory around that reality earned Robert Solow a
1987 Nobel Prize.

Epoch-changing shifts in technology do two inter-
related things: they propel economies, and they introduce
unintended disruptions across society. None of history's
technological disruptions were predicted by economists or
policymakers. But once a disruption is underway, pundits
pile on fast with predictions about implications and
impacts – predictions that are almost always wrong, both
in character and in outcomes.

Now, again, we are at the beginning of a new technological epoch, this one characterized by the infusion of

automation into everything. This transformation comes at a propitious time.

We're in a productivity deficit

For a decade now, America has been in a productivity deficit. (See Figure 2.) By definition, this means that America is under-invested in productivity-driving technologies. Thus, while much has been written about the causes and management of the recent "great recession," one cannot blame automation for the high unemployment rates during this period of anemic growth. Put another way, if automation is eliminating jobs, we would see a collateral *increase* in productivity, because businesses invest in automation only if it improves productivity; that's the whole point.

Spending on new productivity-driving technology happens at the confluence of two forces. First, financial, tax and regulatory conditions must be favorable for accessing and deploying capital. Technology always entails capital spending. Second, the new technologies are purchased at scale only when they are sufficiently mature. Maturity isn't just a cost metric. High costs can be justified if outcomes yield greater benefits. The key signal of maturity is when a technology becomes relatively easy to adopt within the organizational and human practicalities of any enterprise.

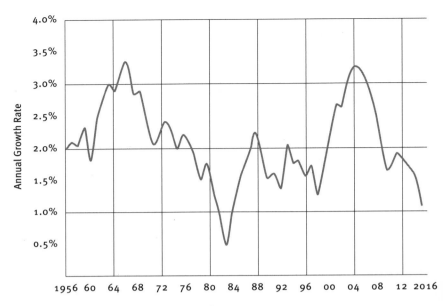

Figure 2   U.S. Productivity Growth, 1956–2016
Source: U.S. Bureau of Labor Statistics

Back in the 1970s, economists were puzzled by a productivity collapse similar to our current one. No productivity gains were apparent from the then recent mainframe computer revolution, a time, incidentally, when IBM enjoyed a dominant market share matched today only by the likes of Amazon's dominance in Cloud hardware. Few experts – arguably no one – in the 1970s foresaw what would emerge in the decades that followed.

The 1976 economic report to Congress by the Council

of Economic Advisers (chaired by Alan Greenspan) did not contain the word "computer." Missing the computer revolution in economic forecasts at that time was understandable, but no small error.

The systemic economic and societal impact of computing would not manifest itself until later, with the emergence of broadly distributed personal computing. Similarly, the associated employment of millions of people would not show up until the explosive growth of personal computing and the rise of firms like Intel and Microsoft.

Now, in the early part of the 21st century, it is clear from the trends seen in Figure 2 that the nation is at or near the bottom of a productivity cycle. Today's state of automation and AI is no more broadly distributed than computing was in the mainframe era (1960–1980). The next incarnation of productivity-driving computing technology has yet to be democratized. When it is, we can expect a surge in productivity and economic growth for America.

Productivity growth solves a lot of problems

There is one thing we know about economies: while robust growth can't solve all of society's problems, it can go a long way toward ameliorating many of them. But many economists and forecasters have been claiming that America is in a "new normal" in which GDP growth is going to hover around an anemic 2% a year for the foreseeable future.

As every economics student learns, rising productivity is precisely what creates economic growth. This is not debatable. Where there are debates, they center on what policies will best ensure productivity and whether, for example, bureaucrats can stimulate or direct the emergence of technologies that increase productivity. Only a small uptick in productivity is required to restore the U.S. economy to an average of 3% to 4% annual GDP growth.

At a 3.5% annual growth rate, by 2028 the U.S. economy would be $3.6 trillion bigger than one that staggered along at a 2% rate. The latter is the growth rate assumed by the Congressional Budget Office (CBO) for calculating the deficit and other amounts. The CBO, by default, assumes that technology-driven productivity advances won't emerge; this assumption requires myopia, a lot of hubris, or both. A nearly $4 trillion increase in the GDP would bring extra wealth equivalent to adding a California plus a Texas to the U.S. economy. It also would represent a cumulative addition to the economy about equal to the federal debt.

So we find ourselves at a curious place in history. If the automation-kills-jobs thesis is correct, then America's future is one – the claim goes – in which robots and AI make us richer overall but with most work found in the "knowledge economy," while jobs disappear everywhere else. Hence we see the resurrection of the idea of a Universal Basic Income (UBI), funded by taxing either robots or those companies deploying AI – that is, invisible virtual robots in the Cloud. The end-of-work adherents argue that a UBI is needed to support the "inevitable" rise of a permanent unemployed class. Is there any precedent in history for such an outcome?

Productivity and employment have grown together for 130 years

We know two things about the effect of the myriad technological changes over the past 130 years. The first is that continual and often profound advances in labor-saving productivity have boosted the economy so much that per capita wealth has reached unprecedented heights. The second is that despite all that "labor saving," about 95% of willing and able people have, on average, continued to be employed. In other words, the unemployment rate has remained essentially unchanged at about 5% for all of those 130 years, episodically fluctuating due to cyclical recessions. (See Figure 3.)

If labor-saving technology were a net job destroyer, the unemployment rate should have been growing inexorably over history. But it hasn't. MIT economist David Autor has been particularly eloquent on the apparent paradox of

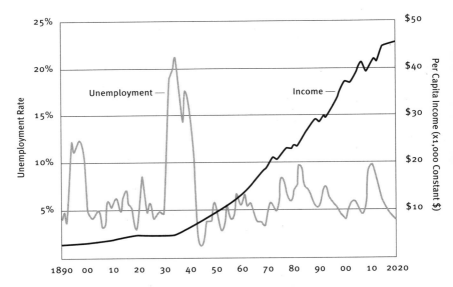

Figure 3   130 Years of U.S. Economic Growth
Source: Federal Reserve Bank of St. Louis

more employment despite unrelenting advances in labor-reducing technologies, observing that, with regard to the prospects for employment growth, "the fundamental threat is not technology per se but misgovernance."

Of course, where and how most people are employed has changed. Farming, the most commonly noted example of vanishing employment, accounted for 40% of jobs in the pre-industrial era, compared to only 2% today. In the 1960s, the early days of modern automation saw a rapid decline in automobile-manufacturing jobs, despite the huge boom in automakers' output. Consider a more recent example, the 1976 introduction of a practical word processor by Wang Laboratories. (Wang invented modern word processing and utterly dominated that market into the early 1980s but was unable to navigate the creative destruction of the burgeoning PC industry, filing for bankruptcy in 1992.) Word processing quickly supplanted the old corporate "typing pool" and most secretarial jobs, which, at that time, were mostly held by women. This clerical labor-saving device, it bears noting, came on the scene around the time of a huge increase in the number of women in the workforce. Again, as the data show, neither general nor female unemployment soared.

We saw the same pattern with the introduction of spreadsheet and computer-graphics programs, which eliminated a lot of number-crunching and drafting jobs. Those new labor-saving tools, along with many other similar technological advances of the 1980s and 1990s, were contemporaneous with overall U.S. employment *growth*.

Nonetheless, episodic recessions are inevitable in any economy. Technology cannot change the cyclical nature of markets. Blaming unemployment on labor-saving automation – rather than "misgovernance," incompetence, shortsightedness or other human frailties – during economic downturns is an old tradition.

In 1934, during the Great Depression, the left-leaning Industrial Workers of the World (IWW) published a report "establishing clearly" that "the machine has added to unemployment," blaming unemployment on both capitalism and engineers as "capitalist tools." The IWW pointed to a nearly fourfold drop from 1910 to 1930 in labor-hours per automobile manufactured and a sevenfold decline from 1900 to 1930 in labor-hours per ton of steel. The IWW also noted, but with less alarm (perhaps because it involved farmers, not factory workers), that technology had reduced the number of labor-hours needed to produce America's 1929 wheat output to a hundredth of what would have been required 74 years earlier.

In the early 1960s, America was just starting to recover from three recessions over the previous seven years. A self-appointed group of experts, including Nobel laureates in science and economics, issued a report asserting that, with the new kinds of automation then in evidence on Detroit's automobile production lines, the "traditional link between jobs and incomes is being broken." Today, it's easy to forget – because of the "presentism" inevitable with historical myopia – just how surprised people were by the technological leaps that followed World War II. Those rapid changes fueled an enthusiastic media and a gullible public to imagine the imminence of flying cars, colonies on the moon and atomic-powered aircraft.

President John F. Kennedy, circa 1961, created an Office of Automation and Manpower within the Department of Labor because of the need to address, as he put it, "the major domestic challenge of the Sixties: to maintain full employment at a time when automation, of course, is replacing men." In a "Special Message" to Congress, he proposed that the government should help "workers displaced by technological change" and that there should be "readjustment allowances" for the displaced, as well as new vocational and skills-training programs and relocation assistance.

Following that, President Lyndon B. Johnson convened a Blue Ribbon commission to study the effects of "Technology, Automation, and Economic Progress." Even though that commission concluded that technology did not threaten employment, it nonetheless recommended an "insurance" policy against such a possibility, proposing that the government create "a guaranteed minimum income for each family." Perhaps those proposing a UBI today should name it the Kennedy-Johnson Tax.

Policymakers reasonably worry about the moral and political challenges of helping those left behind by dislocations in labor markets, an important issue we revisit later in this essay. Hence the modern emergence of many types of safety-net programs, from unemployment benefits to retraining assistance. Technology, of course, *does* eliminate jobs in specific activities: to repeat, that is the point of automation when it produces the same or a superior outcome or product at a lower cost.

But the thesis being proffered by today's alarmists is that there is something fundamentally different about *digital* automation and software in the form of AI and anthropomorphic robots. The end-of-work adherents implicitly or explicitly believe that new labor-saving technologies are so powerful that they will finally reverse the course of history that has seen technology propel both wealth and work.

Amara's Law helps us imagine the future

As should be clear by now, forecasting future employment is anchored in technology forecasting, a quasi-profession in which speculation often runs ahead and even independent of reality.

Imagining usefully foreseeable technology is more difficult than one might expect. The key is to figure out not just *what* is likely to happen, but, more important, *when* it is likely to happen at scales that are meaningful.

Stanford computer scientist Roy Amara deserves credit for observing, a half-century ago, that forecasters tend to overestimate technological change in the short term and underestimate it in the long term. What Amara's Law captures is a common failure to appreciate the time it takes for

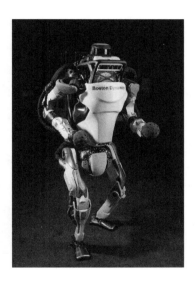

Figure 4   The Enduring Pursuit of the Anthropomorphic Robot
LEFT: Inventor W. H. Richards and "George" the Robot, 1932
RIGHT: Boston Dynamics Atlas, DARPA 2017

The word "robot" originated in 1920 with Czech playwright Karel Čapek, whose play Rossum's Universal Robots *imagined machines taking over manual labor. Čapek derived the word "robot" from the Czech "robota," which translates to forced labor or drudgery.*

engineering development to make a new technology practical enough to reach an "inflection point," the point at which it enters widespread use, creating a growth pattern seen in the famous hockey-stick curve that so many entrepreneurs use in their forecasts.

Everything looks like an overnight success after the inflection point. Andy Grove, Intel's storied CEO, frequently wrote about the critical importance of understanding the magnitude of the engineering challenges and thus the time needed to reach inflection – and how often forecasters ignored the long period of pre-inflection developments. History demonstrates that, when it comes to major technological dislocations, most forecasts get both the "what" and the "when" wrong.

It took, for example, 20 years from the invention of the automobile to the development of a practical automobile, the Model T, and then nearly 20 more years before automobile sales took off, permanently changing the world. It took nearly 20 years from first fission to the first commercial nuclear reactor; nuclear-power technology turns out to be so difficult that we're still waiting for an inflection point.

Similarly, getting to the moon seemed to happen very quickly, but it was 40 years after the invention of the rocket before Kennedy issued the challenge and then almost another decade before the 1969 landing. And the inflection point – putting lots of people in outer space to work or vacation (the dreams of Jeff Bezos' Blue Origin and Elon Musk's SpaceX) – is turning out to take far longer.

Even the often-vaunted rapid pace of computers has followed the same pattern. It was almost 20 years from the first electronic computer until the first practical commercial computers and then another 20 years before the mainframe inflection point. And, it was 20 years from the equivalent of "first fission" for the Internet before Amazon

We see code in the Cloud already disrupting old business models and jobs in law firms, shopping malls, film studios, hotels, newspapers, broadcast TV, finance, and even education.

went public in 1997. Nearly another 20 years passed before it became obvious that e-commerce was reaching an inflection point.

Schumpeter's "creative destruction" in retail is much in discussion now. Sears, one iconic example, has seen its hardware-centric enterprise collapse in the last decade, while Amazon's has expanded 20-fold and is still growing. But even the most bullish forecasts about e-commerce and the Internet's dawn circa the 1990s (the "you've got mail" days) did not envision the nature and scope of that trend or, more important, the magnitude of the Cloud's hardware infrastructure behind it.

Computers began improving labor productivity among "knowledge workers" some 75 years ago. And thank goodness. British mathematician Alan Turing, one of the fathers of computing, said that were it not for the computer he'd built during World War II it would have taken "100 Britons working eight hours a day on desk calculators 100 years" to crack the Germans' method of encrypting messages. After that feat, roughly 40 years passed until a computer, IBM's Deep Blue, was good enough to trump chess grandmaster Garry Kasparov in 1997. As every computer scientist knows, that accomplishment was one of computational "horsepower" and not a demonstration of true AI, but it made it clear there was a path to AI. Conquering chess, with its astronomically large number of narrowly defined sets of possibilities, while directly derivate from Turing, had been impossible until the underlying hardware reached a new pinnacle.

AI, which has no clearly agreed definition, involves more than mere number-crunching horsepower to solve clearly defined, albeit enormous, problems. AI entails using both hardware and new kinds of software (even new kinds of mathematics) to conquer diffuse and indeterminate problems, more akin to the day-to-day human ability to answer unrelated questions. Similarly, a general-purpose robot, especially an anthropomorphic one, would be fundamentally different from one that did exactly the same task over and over but with more speed (e.g., an automotive production-line robot). A general-purpose robot should be able to open a door, or carry a box, or operate a fire hose, all quite unrelated tasks. Achieving AI or general-purpose robotics involves much more than increasing data-processing speed. It requires foundationally different phenomenology and radically different hardware.

Taxonomy for automation: Code in the Cloud and code in the cobot

Robots are emerging on two distinct tracks: the purely cyber and the cyberphysical (the latter the engineers' term of art). Both involve code: while one resides entirely inside computational machines, the other either becomes, or directly controls, non-computational machines. In the first case, think in terms of Apple's Siri or Amazon's Alexa audio assistant, able to respond (using AI in the Cloud) to natural verbal questions and instructions.

For a cyberphysical example, look to the Da Vinci surgical robot – or, more precisely, "cobot" – or the newly announced Monarch flexible surgical robot, both enabling ultra-precise surgery but still guided by a physician. The term "cobot" (coined by Northwestern University professors Michael Colgate and Edward Peshkin) is applied to robots that are guided by or collaborate with people, as compared to autonomous machines or those operating independently but in parallel with humans.

The equivalent of "first fission" for AI may be recorded by history as the 1997 chess match when Grand Master Garry Kasparov lost to IBM's Deep Blue. It wasn't until 2011, however, that we first saw an inkling of practical use for AI when IBM, as a PR stunt, pitted its Watson AI computer against the best human contestants on the TV game show *Jeopardy* (and won). Now, we see a proliferation of consumer products similar to Alexa and Siri, as well as Watson, used in hospitals as virtual assistants for doctors. The jury is still out on the inflection point, but if the patterns noted earlier hold, it may be only a decade away.

Similarly, history will likely record as "first fission" for autonomous cars the 2004 DARPA (Defense Advanced Research Projects Agency) grand challenge for autonomous vehicles. (Vehicle autonomy has long been a goal of the U.S. military, which created DARPA in 1957.) Today's highly publicized self-driving-car programs nearly all derive from key technologies, features, designs and even many of the professionals themselves associated with that

DARPA contest. Notwithstanding enthusiastic PR and hype, no company has yet achieved true autonomy for its vehicles. Indeed, the accidents that have already occurred with AI-driven vehicles (including the recent tragic pedestrian death at the "hands" of a self-driving Uber) highlight unresolved technical challenges. The 20-year time line from "first fission" to the first commercially viable self-driving car is still a half-dozen years away, possibly more. Then widespread adoption will take yet more time and likely follow the same historical pattern, requiring about two more decades to begin to scale at society-wide levels.

As for useful anthropomorphic robots, we likely saw "first fission" at another DARPA challenge. In a 2015 contest, engineers sought to demonstrate untethered walking robots (most costing well north of $1 million) that could operate in high-risk environments such as firefighting. The goal was to have machines that could literally walk into places designed for humans – but when it would be too dangerous for people – and perform tasks autonomously. Imagine robots putting out a fire in the corridors of a submarine or turning off a hazardous gas leak in the interstices of a chemical plant. The 20-plus-20-year heuristic would situate the inflection point around 2055.

However, long before every inflection point in history, new businesses were created to both manufacture and serve niche applications – and employ people – for the new technologies. By the time of the automobile's inflection point circa 1930, more than 400 automobile companies had arisen (most didn't make it), and millions of cars had been produced. By the circa-1980 personal-computer inflection point, similarly, hundreds of computer companies had emerged and disappeared.

So it is reasonable to be concerned about what will happen before the inflection point when both classes of robots – cyber and cyberphysical – possess true autonomy. For it is the autonomous feature – algorithms that don't require specific instructions – that animates so much excitement and anxiety. The cyber and cyberphysical versions each have very different constraints and paces of evolution. There is far less inertia, both literal and financial, in the pace of growth for purely cyber as compared to cyberphysical systems. It is, in effect and in fact, far easier to build a virtual robot to replace a junior attorney than it is to build a physical robot to replace a journeyman electrician.

Thus we see code in the Cloud already disrupting old business models and jobs in law firms, shopping malls, film studios, hotels, newspapers, broadcast TV, finance, and even education. If we're lucky, algorithms will improve productivity in government services by automating much of the "rote" knowledge work that occupies so many bureaucrats and regulators. All these service-sector domains employ a vast cadre of white-collar professionals. And the service sector, broadly defined, is where we find the vast majority of jobs. (See Figure 5.)

Knowing that machines can replace workers is as old as the wheel. One of the features of today's digital revolution, however, compared to the early ages of automation, is that the march of "creative destruction" involves a different category of worker. The long-ago automation of faraway

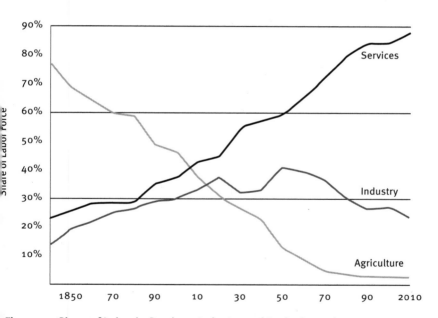

Figure 5   Share of Labor in Services, Industry and Agriculture since 1840
Source: Lebergott, Stanley, National Bureau of Economic Research &
Federal Reserve Bank of St. Louis

We are witnessing the inevitable migration to a knowledge-centric economy, but one that can be – should be – about as dependent on manufacturing for employment as it was in the past.

factories and farms, which continues today, disrupted the agricultural and blue-collar workforces. Now, automation is starting to sweep through the service sectors in city centers and disrupt white-collar jobs. Having already changed the "means of farming" and the "means of production," technology is finally getting around to changing the "means of management" of activities in the service sectors.

No wonder pundits and members of the white-collar media obsessively write and talk about the "end of work." Doubtless many fear it's the end of *their* work this time.

America has always been service-dominated, but manufacturing remains critical

Before we turn to the issue of labor productivity in services, consider whether it's likely that the share of labor in industry will, as is widely claimed, inevitably follow the agricultural trajectory down to a single-digit-percentage share.

Alexander Hamilton's words contained in his 1791 "Report on Manufactures" are still true: "Not only the wealth, but the independence and security of a Country, appear to be materially connected with the prosperity of manufactures." This reality does not mean, however, that manufacturing is the primary source of employment. More people have been employed in *services* than in industry since the days when Hamilton wrote those words. (See Figure 5.)

The convention of categorizing the economy and jobs into the three domains of agriculture, manufacturing and services distorts our ability to understand economic, technology and employment trends. Within the services category, a hospital is as different from a retail business as either of those is from a factory, and all are equally different from agriculture. So let's break the categories down. A look at Bureau of Economic Analysis data shows that manufacturing is the biggest sector of the economy. (See Figure 6.) In fact, manufacturing is 50% bigger than the number-two category, professional services.

Furthermore, manufacturing accounts for 45% of exports and 70% of all private-sector spending on R&D. In employment terms, as is well documented in the economic literature, manufacturing employment has an outsized benefit for the rest of the economy. A dollar of wages paid in one sector leads to spill-over benefits in the rest of the economy, a so-called multiplier effect. One dollar paid to a service worker generates 80 cents of economic activity elsewhere;

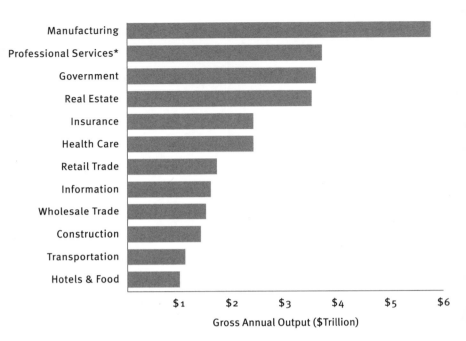

Figure 6 America's Top 12 Economic Sectors
*Includes scientific, technical, management, administrative services,
design of computer systems*
Source: Bureau of Economic Analysis

a dollar paid for a manufacturing job has $4 of spill-over.

The central fact of manufacturing's powerful economic multiplier argues for policymakers to think hard about how to help, not hurt, that sector. And this multiplier also makes clear that encouraging labor productivity in manufacturing – to increase global competitiveness – has an outsized benefit for wealth and jobs in the rest of the domestic economy.

The post-industrial myth for manufacturing jobs

Harvard sociologist Daniel Bell predicted the shift to an information-led economy in 1973 in his influential book, *The Coming of Post-Industrial Society*. He proposed that societies naturally migrate from agriculture to industrial pursuits and then to a knowledge economy. Bell's hypothesis has been widely interpreted to mean that factory jobs will follow farm work down to a single-digit-percentage share of overall employment. The problem is the data so far don't support that derivative proposition.

But first it's important to note that the underlying employment data are distorted by a categorization challenge as the structure of the economy changes. Tasks that are integral to manufacturing are increasingly miscategorized as "services." For example, if a product's final assembly – unequivocally a manufacturing process – takes place in a warehouse (a feature that Amazon and UPS offer), those employees are counted in "services." By one estimate, there are already 30,000 such U.S. warehouse manufacturing jobs. This kind of outsourcing is happening with all manner of so-called services, from trucking to IT.

The line between services and manufacturing is particularly blurred by the rapid growth in use of off-site Cloud data tools (instead of on-site computing) for design and operations, which shifts the associated employment into services. This fast-growing category of labor, which the Commerce Department designates as "digitally delivered services," also confounds conventional trade balance calculations. The economically efficient merging of "services" and manufacturing has just begun.

Categorization errors aside, the overall trends do illustrate that, as wealth grows in industrialized nations, the share of a population employed in manufacturing first rises, then reaches a plateau and, for most nations, slowly declines. (That decline, however, doesn't necessarily need to continue, as Germany and Japan have demonstrated over the past decade.) But, in the many studies on this subject, one doesn't find economic maturity leading to a sudden collapse in a country's manufacturing share of employment. The exception? The past decade or so in America, where, as has been widely reported, manufacturing's share of employment dropped precipitously. So what happened?

In part, the U.S. manufacturing sector has been losing global market share, especially to China. But that doesn't explain the plunge in the number of Americans employed in factories over the past decade or so. And the data show that manufacturers' overall spending on information technology *decreased* over that period. This latter fact doesn't support the idea that algorithms are taking over manufacturing jobs. IT spending as a share of revenue in manufacturing, energy, chemicals and food-processing sectors is one-fifth to one-half that in the information-centric sectors of media, banking, education and insurance.

Aside from the rise of China, a non-trivial competitive factor, the single biggest change over the past decade or so has been an astonishing rise in the size of America's regulatory state, the majority of which is directed at the industrial and manufacturing sectors. Between 2006 and 2016, the number of federal regulators, as well as the budget devoted to regulating, doubled.

There are now 300,000 federal regulators spending $60 billion a year on activities that (a) mainly target industry and (b) impede economic growth. There was no safety, environmental or structural crisis in the American economy a decade ago that could justify such a radical increase in the regulatory burden. In fact, with the rise of lightly regulated China, policymakers could not have hobbled American industry at a worse time.

American companies, overall, now spend an average of $10,000 per year per employee on regulatory compliance. Meanwhile large manufacturers spend double that. And the per-employee burden for small manufacturers is nearly double that again. It should be no surprise that America's manufacturing output, as well as its employment growth, has slowed.

Unfavorable tax treatment has recently also inhibited the expansion of domestic manufacturing. This was (finally) remedied in late 2017, when tax cuts brought America's corporate tax rates back into line with Western norms. But the radical rise of the regulatory state has been an equal, if not greater, drag on manufacturing, and a gratuitous one at that.

Even in its beaten-down condition, U.S. manufacturing employs more than three times as many people as the information sector. Census data show that the entire information sector accounts for only 5% of national employment, with a flat trend. And manufacturing accounts for three times as much of the GDP as does the information sector.

Implementing tax and regulatory policies favorable to capital spending (technology is always capital-intensive) will lead to investment in new manufacturing technologies, especially automation and IT. Such investment will make businesses more productive and more competitive.

Knowledge jobs are not replacing manufacturing ones; rather, they are becoming an increasingly integral part of manufacturing. In this regard, Daniel Bell was right. We are witnessing the inevitable migration to a knowledge-centric economy, but one that can be – should be – about as dependent on manufacturing for employment as it was in the past. The end result will be fewer labor-hours per new product produced, but far more output and – absent "misgovernance" – net new jobs, especially ones that had not previously existed.

Blue-collar bots

The opportunity for American manufacturing is visible in the global trends. The rate of adoption of next-generation industrial robots points to the opportunity for more productivity yet to be tapped.

There are already about two million industrial robots in the world today, and most forecasts predict that number will soon double. The new U.S. tax policies, which accelerate depreciation for capital, will likely accelerate American businesses' adoption of this capital-intensive mechanized technology.

So far, two U.S. industrial sectors – the automotive sector and the computer and electrical equipment sector – have purchased twice as many robots as all the other sectors combined. The metals, chemicals, food and other industries have been slow to enlist robots because of the complexities and varieties of the tasks involved. Whereas the nature of automobile fabrication, with its constrained and highly repetitive tasks, lends itself easily to automation, many other industrial activities are more amorphous and resemble the kind of open-ended variable tasks common in the service sectors. But as robots become more capable, more flexible, more cooperative (cobots) and less expensive, the number of robots in use in all industrial sectors will grow – especially under the earlier noted new tax laws.

Recently released data show the first indications of the new trend. Some $2 billion was spent last year to put 34,000 more robots into U.S. industrial services, a healthy 10% one-year growth rate. And the vast majority of the robots purchased were for non-automotive manufacturing.

Manufacturing 2.0

Improvements in American manufacturing competitiveness could not come at a better time. The global demand for manufactured goods is on the cusp of the greatest expansion in history. Massive increases in demand are coming not only for more of today's goods, but also for entirely new kinds of products currently in development.

Measured in money (not percentages, since it's the quantity of money that directly determines buying power), the world's GDP is forecasted to expand by nearly twice as much over the next 20 years as it did in the past 20. This means at least twice as much growth in demand for everything from cars and aircraft, to tractors and chemicals, to clothes and computers. All of these things will be fabricated, all of them will be more complex than in the past and, thus, all of them will migrate to more information-intensive production systems.

Add to this the emergence of entirely new types of products yet to be manufactured. The rise of the Internet of Things (IoT), which will piggyback the existing Internet – much as containerization rode an existing infrastructure – requires the manufacturing of trillions of sensors and "smart" devices. One of the biggest and perhaps most significant IoT markets will entail healthcare. In the near future, bio-electronics and transient electronics (think in terms of usefully "consumable" computers) will likely lead to an industry as big as today's $3 trillion silicon-electronics sector.

In addition, researchers and developers are pioneering practical uses for new types of exotic materials, not least among them graphene and carbon fibers, as well as so-called metamaterials (materials that exhibit properties that don't exist naturally). And even though it still seems fanciful, dozens of firms, from start-up operations to industry giant Airbus, are developing air taxis, which means that soon yet another new industry will emerge to manufacture them. Finally, if the private-sector space entrepreneurs are right, and commercial space travel becomes a real industry and not a niche, there will necessarily emerge yet more new manufacturing enterprises to produce all the specialized hardware.

With all of the above, the low-cost producer has an enormous advantage as always. For any manufacturer, competitiveness and growth are served best not by cheap labor but by superior technology. Fortunately, the manufacturing sector has long exhibited the power to put new tools to work once they become practical. The technologies surrounding robotics, in particular, are rapidly advancing for manufacturing applications. The same technologies are now also reaching a kind of tipping point for use in the service industries.

The coming robotification of services

Venture-capital investment offers a window into the kinds of technology that will drive future productivity gains. Here we see, in the CBInsights tracking of robot investments, that service-oriented – rather than industrial – applications dominate, with 80% of the $3 billion of venture capital in the past four years put to work on next-generation robots.

Investors made bets on companies developing robots for retail, warehouse, delivery, laboratory, educational, surgical, hospital, rehab, safety, security, environmental monitoring and "social" applications. Clearly, innovators and investors think that services represent a great opportunity for success.

Infusing software *into* hardware – to make true cyberphysical systems, such that they become functionally, invisibly and reliably part of the world of atoms – is chal-

For any manufacturer, competitiveness and growth are served best not by cheap labor but by superior technology.

lenging. Unlike the purely cyber world, the physical world has things like inertia, friction, gravity and non-linear random events, all with serious safety implications. The real (as opposed to virtual) world cannot tolerate the equivalent of frozen screens, reboots, video jitter or iterations of software upgrades to clean up sloppy code rushed to market. But cyberphysical technologies are improving rapidly, and we have already seen "first fission." But long before we see practical general-purpose robots, we will see commercially viable task-specific ones for applications across the service sectors.

A proliferation of prototypes can be seen already, including some early commercial products for applications ranging from warehouse and delivery services, to firefighting and rescue work, to the Pentagon's robotic "mule" program for carrying heavy gear for soldiers. The "mule" program has slowed, in large measure because such general-purpose machines remain both too expensive and too noisy in the field. The robot equivalent of the Model A has yet to be sold.

However, practical Model A's, if not Model T's, are already in use in homes, hospitals and warehouses, where comparatively light tasks and proximity to power sources make battery-powered robots viable. The more specific and narrow the task, the simpler the cyberphysical challenges and the less expensive the machine. Six years ago, Amazon spent $700 million to acquire robot-maker Kiva for its wheeled, turtle-like, pallet-carrying warehouse robot. And Amazon has been sponsoring an annual contest to see whether robots can grab jumbled products from a bin and put them on a shelf.

Other types of service-specific machines are starting to appear, still mostly prototypes but some commercially available. While surgical cobots continue to be a significant early market, we see applications for service-related tasks in security, safety and environmental monitoring and assessment, general-purpose cleaning, hospital disinfection and self-driving wheelchairs.

A total of 10 million service robots are already sold annually around the world, though 80% are robotic vacuum cleaners, with most of the balance either robotic lawn mowers or light-duty drones. The forecast for 60 million low-cost service robots sold annually before 2030 anticipates engineers succeeding in conquering performance and cost challenges in a broad range of applications. But the inflection point is now in sight for a trend that began with history's first modern household washing machine a century ago. The emerging panoply of service robots will be directed at all applications, not just domestic chores and entertainment.

Better labor productivity can bring down soaring healthcare costs

Improved labor productivity is long overdue for many services, especially healthcare. As tech analyst Bret Swanson has usefully summarized, over the past 15 years, healthcare productivity – value added per labor-hour – has remained stagnant, while productivity in physical industries has improved by about 15% and productivity in digital industries has improved by 50%. (See Figure 7.)

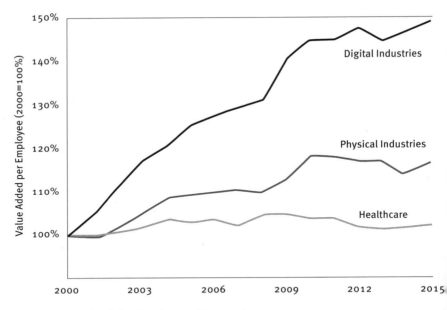

Figure 7 Productivity: Leaders and Laggards
Source: Entropy Economics

The absence of real progress in service labor productivity is clearly visible in the net result. Consider the changes in cost of goods versus cost of services in America over the past 20 years. While the prices of childcare, education and, especially, medical and hospital services have increased by as much as four times the rate of inflation, the real costs associated with the production of physical things (e.g., cars, computers, furniture and food) have either decreased dramatically or, at least, not outpaced inflation. That's the magic of productivity gains, which most service-centric activities have yet to experience.

It's an old maxim in economics: if you want more of something, make it cheaper. The inverse also applies: rising costs depress people's ability to acquire the desired product or service and collaterally depress the potential for (productive) employment growth in the industries providing those products and services.

Data: The fuel for boosting service-sector productivity

Even though all the key components are now available or rapidly maturing, we are still in early days for the new classes of physical robots that will boost productivity across the range of service activities. The engineering challenges of cyberphysical systems, where software meets steel (or carbon fiber) in real time, are daunting and necessarily multidisciplinary. Meanwhile, AI – the virtual robot – is already viable, maturing rapidly and on the cusp of inflection. Computer code in the Cloud can use voice recognition to answer questions, help perform handy personal tasks and increasingly tackle complex real-world information-centric tasks, from reading patients' X-rays to advising physicians on diagnoses.

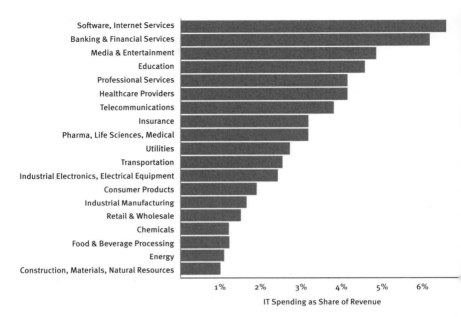

Software, Internet Services					
Banking & Financial Services					
Media & Entertainment					
Education					
Professional Services					
Healthcare Providers					
Telecommunications					
Insurance					
Pharma, Life Sciences, Medical					
Utilities					
Transportation					
Industrial Electronics, Electrical Equipment					
Consumer Products					
Industrial Manufacturing					
Retail & Wholesale					
Chemicals					
Food & Beverage Processing					
Energy					
Construction, Materials, Natural Resources					

IT Spending as Share of Revenue

Figure 8 Business Spending on IT
Source: IDC

Service-related activities are fundamentally more
information-centric than hardware-centric and are thus
more amenable to rapid adoption of knowledge automation. In fact, business spending on IT reflects that reality:
finance, education and insurance businesses spend two to
four times (as a share of expenses) as much on IT as do
hardware-centric industries such as manufacturing, chemicals and energy. (See Figure 8.) Huge sectors of the economy are still under-investing in IT and have thus yet to
reap the productivity gains possible.

But, by definition, the algorithms on which AI relies must be fed data. For those businesses that are early adopters of AI itself, not just other features of IT, a recent survey illustrates that the applications tend to be focused in areas where there are a lot of data and where those data are relatively easy to access. (See Figure 9.)

The newly popular intelligent virtual assistants (IVAs), such as Amazon's Alexa and Google's Voice, are virtual robots for consumers, providing a service based on an AI

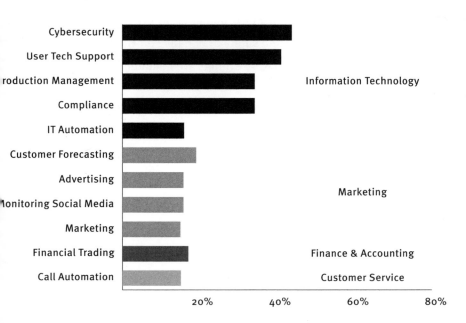

Figure 9   Activities Where Companies Report Using AI (Worldwide)
Source: Tata Consulting Services

engine in the Cloud. These personal IVAs, already expected to be a $2 billion business by 2020, recognize and respond in natural language using the wealth of public information on the Internet. They can also interface with relatively simple "smart" devices in a home (e.g., a thermostat, a garage door). Many IVAs provide services or entertainment without displacing human labor, since most people don't have human assistants.

IVA technology is migrating into cars and toys, the latter including educational features. But to put IVAs and AI more broadly into service environments, where they can improve productivity and safety or enhance on-the-job training and education, three things are needed:

1.   Data about people and the things people use

2.   A connection to access that data

3.   The capacity to process unprecedented quantities of data

The last two features constitute infrastructure (more about that shortly). Data acquisition is the key – without data, virtual robots are as blind as physical robots without vision systems and other sensors to navigate their environs.

The development and deployment of sensors capable of measuring specific, real-time and minute features of objects and people in nearly every aspect of society has reached an inflection point. The market for "smart" sensors has exploded, with billions of devices in use today and trillions on track for deployment in another decade. Venture investing, again one of the bellwethers for the velocity of emerging technology, is seeing more than $2 billion a year directed at IoT sensors. "Smart" sensors can generate useful data about nearly anything, from retail inventory control and shipping to precise body functions and health measurements (real-time blood sugar, heart rate, tri-glycerides, etc.).

The magnitude and character of data traffic on the Internet is expanding at an unprecedented rate. The amount of data moving *daily* on the Internet will, in a few years, exceed *annual* traffic of a decade ago. And all that data traffic has already started to shift toward economy-boosting, labor-saving productivity. Although today, Internet traffic is dominated by various forms of entertainment — and entertainment traffic is expected to grow 4,000% over the coming decade — productivity-related data, especially in and around the myriad services essential to society, will account for triple the Internet traffic associated with entertainment by 2025. (See Figure 10.)

And while it is true that every nation can eventually benefit from technology invented anywhere in the world,

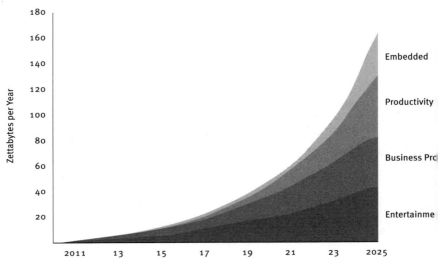

Figure 10   Internet Data Traffic, 2010–2025 (Projected)
Source: Cisco

early leaders in technology often gain sustainable advantages. It is thus notable that America is home to more than three-fourths of the top 100 AI start-ups, with $12 billion of collective private investment thus far.

The hyperscale data infrastructure and ubiquitous productivity

Familiar companies like Uber and Airbnb epitomize some of the types of efficiencies currently emerging from data and connectivity that will someday happen across all service classes. The essence of the "magic" of Uber is in providing *information* about service users to service providers and vice versa: Uber links party A, who is "here and needs a ride" (located by a GPS sensor), to party B, who is "nearby and available to drive you." The Airbnb platform offers the same economic arbitrage between parties looking to rent and parties looking for a place to stay. Information arbitrage is a powerful economic lubricant and can add value from under-utilized people and assets. But it requires a ubiquitous existing hardware infrastructure. All the emerging data-arbitrage businesses are able to utilize the massive Cloud computing and wireless communications networks that have been built by others.

As noted earlier, two of history's iconic examples of the symbiosis between innovation and new infrastructures are (a) the steam engines and railroads that made (among many other things) Sears and Roebuck possible and (b) the modern ships and ports that made containerization possible. Both those infrastructure-enabled productivity revolutions led to more prosperity and, in the end, far greater productivity, which, derivatively, led to more overall employment.

The inevitability of the rapid emergence of deep labor-saving productivity in services is visible in the magnitude of infrastructure *hardware* being built to store and process the flood of data. Hundreds of hyperscale and millions of small data centers connected by glass fibers and high-speed wireless networks form a seamless web that literally encompasses the planet.

Few people putting gasoline in a car – the technology that automated mobility – have any concept of the scale of hardware and engineering talent inherent in extracting petroleum from 30,000 feet below the surface and delivering it seamlessly and affordably. Even fewer people understand the similar feat of delivering "refined" data from deep within the mountains of data available. At the core of the infrastructure are thousands of data centers, many the size of a city block. More computing power than existed on Earth in the 1970s is now contained in a few square feet of each such building. The new hyperscale infrastructure – which would be impossible for most businesses to acquire, install, maintain and operate on their own – democratizes access to algorithms and AI with a utility-like convenience and cost.

A sense of the scale of this new infrastructure is revealed in the magnitude of global spending on IT hardware, now about $3 trillion per year. This figure rivals global spending by the oil and gas industry on energy-production hardware. Cloud companies are building billion-dollar data centers faster than oil companies are building billion-dollar offshore platforms.

48

More than a dozen corporations are competing to build and dominate the new hyperscale infrastructure, and thousands more are emerging that use that infrastructure to provide new or better services. Once again looking at venture-capital spending, of the more than 200 companies that are each valued at over $1 billion – the so-called unicorns of private venture-funded companies – more than 80% are focused on services, from financial and retail to travel and healthcare.

Ubiquitous data and ambient computing lead to the third information era

America is entering a third information era. The first information era spanned roughly 1960 to 1980, after the inflection point that led to the commercialization of mainframe computers. That was followed by the era that saw the rise of personal computing and the Internet. We now stand at the cusp of the era of ambient computing and AI – used everywhere, for everything; embedded within things, machines, systems, services and even people. We can chart the trajectory of each information era in the share of the GDP devoted to spending on IT equipment and software. (See Figure 11.)

It may be time to update the iconic observation made

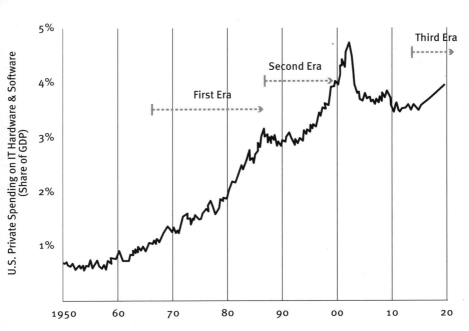

Figure 11 The Third Era: From Mainframe to Personal to Ambient Computing
Source: St. Louis FRED, IT Equip and Software & IDC forecast

by Nobel Prize–winning economist Robert Solow. Remarking in 1987 on lagging employment due to slow productivity growth, he said, "You can see the computer age everywhere but in the productivity statistics." Today one could replace "computer age" with "artificial intelligence." As the earlier data series illustrate, despite media popularizations and some isolated early examples, the era of useful AI is only now starting to emerge, with new classes of practical robots visible on the horizon.

Spending specifically on AI, the pinnacle of the software pyramid, has risen from near zero a few years ago to $2 billion annually and is projected to reach $40 billion a year by 2025. Most of this spending is centered on the hardware for building out the physical infrastructure – in effect, the invisible robots in the Cloud. Over the coming decade, 60% of the forecasted growth in spending on AI will involve hardware, 30% will involve services and just 10% will involve software. While AI will be first put to work mainly in the service sector, all the necessary hardware will be produced in the manufacturing sector. Uber, Amazon and all the rest of the tech intermediaries still depend on some business somewhere to dig up and process minerals, produce energy using huge machines, and fabricate products (cars, robots, semiconductors, boxes, books, etc.).

Of particular note in this transformation, running in parallel with the hyperscale build-out, is the emergence of a new AI infrastructure involving "digital twins." A "digital twin" is a supercomputer's digital model of a machine, a system or even a person that can be compared in real

Of course, educators and employers are eager to have access to people who are familiar with technology, but many of the skills they're seeking don't require a STEM degree.

time to an actual business operation, manufacturing process or human, using highly granular real-time data gathered by sensors embedded on or inside the physical-world counterpart. The digital twin uses that data to analyze and forecast the state of health of its real-world analogue. AI and "machine learning" software, especially digital simulacrums, require incredibly powerful supercomputers: so-called high-performance computers (HPCs). HPCs are another type of IT hardware that is being democratized both for on-site use (where latency and privacy are critical) and for remote use housed within data centers.

Digital twins can do more than bring efficiency and productivity to supply chains or machines; they promise radical improvements for complex systems or processes including, not least, for healthcare and medical procedures. In principle, with sufficiently granular information, a digital twin could predict a particular medication's impact down to the cellular level. While what has been termed the "virtual physiological human" remains aspirational, other service-related and manufacturing processes are already viable. Adoption of this technology is in the early stages. At the beginning of 2018, only 4% of manufacturing companies had operational virtual twins, but almost 30% said they planned to start trials in the coming 12 months.

Software, productivity and jobs grow together

Will the data explosion and the rise of democratized software destroy the long historic correlation between enhanced productivity and job creation? Put in different terms: could it be that *software*-derived productivity will have a different impact on employment than the *hardware*-derived productivity that has been the hallmark of earlier eras?

The recent studies that forecast net declines in employment are based on models and assumptions. While the outcomes have the appearance of precision – with specific numbers associated with specific kinds of employment – all reflect nothing more than analysts' best guesses about complex social, economic and technological dynamics. And all invariably ignore the serendipitous emergence of new kinds of products, companies and jobs. They make, in effect, the dawn-of-the-automobile-era error in overestimating the jobs that would be lost from the horse-and-buggy era. They miss how society will transform and what will follow. To state what should be obvious: automobile-era labor efficiency is astoundingly better than it was in the era of the horse and buggy. Or, put inversely, automobiles radically reduced the labor-hours required per person-mile of transportation. But, with that transformation, employment expanded.

In the future, with healthcare AI, for example, the advent of, say, a system that could predict autism in infants would be enormously beneficial (both morally and economically, in the calculus of long-term healthcare costs). It also wouldn't displace any labor, since no one can, or is, doing that "job." Similarly, robotic exoskeletons for rehabilitation (one firm recently received FDA approval for such), or for the infirm or paraplegics, would bring unmitigated benefits and displace only a small number of people who act as full-time assistants to the disabled. We can expect – indeed, we should hope for – far more automation in such domains, as well as activities such as cleaning and sterilization in hospitals.

Consider another indicative example, the recent introduction of robots that can perform the particularly hazardous task of stripping paint from aircraft. Automation of such jobs not only lowers costs, but also reduces risks (and, again for the economists, reduces associated healthcare costs) in types of work that people might want to avoid in the first place.

As seen in the diffusion of IVAs for physician diagnoses, or cobots to help in surgery or ambulatory care and rehab, the emergence of these types of knowledge services across the field of healthcare is now inevitable. These developments are timely, because healthcare is a huge part of the economy already, and demographics of aging dictate that share can only grow. Automation not only will democratize healthcare and create new classes of services, but – more important – will allow much of those services to migrate from expensive and often hazardous institutional settings into people's homes. Greater productivity and quality, with lower costs, will be welcome.

Rather than guess how all such automation, and other similar applications, will impact employment, we can get an actual indication of likely trends based on the software infusion that has already happened in the past two decades.

The rise of the modern era of enterprise software for both services and industries (1997–2012) saw the emergence of many of today's iconic software companies. And while we are still in early days for most industries, an analysis across dozens of industries over that period shows that, in terms of software spending as a share of inputs, more software was correlated with an overall *increase* in employment. (See Figure 12.)

Figure 12 also illustrates that, especially with low levels of software spending, there are mixed results for employment growth. One can thus cherry-pick an outcome from the diversity of data to find anecdotes that show that

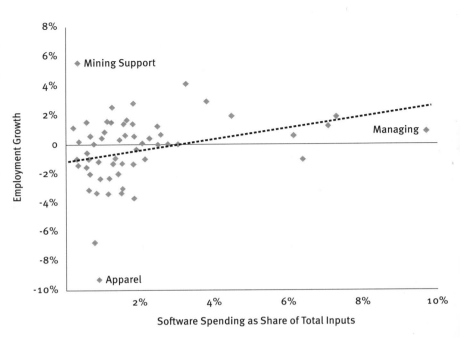

Figure 12 Software Spending vs. Employment Growth, 1997–2012
Source: Software & Information Industry Association (SIIA)

software has caused net job losses. As the data show, a number of businesses (e.g., apparel stores) saw a small uptick in software spending associated with a decline in employment, even when other businesses (e.g., mining) saw an increase. But, as Figure 2 illustrated, America is in a productivity deficit, so it is more reasonable to look to the part of the trends in Figure 12 in which software spending rose more rapidly (as a share of inputs). There we see employment *gains* become the norm.

Bureau of Economic Analysis (BEA) data provide another way to look at these trends over the same period, by correlating jobs with overall labor-productivity changes rather than software spending. While there are other ways to improve labor productivity (e.g., better training), the record shows that spending on software was an important driver in improving business operations from 2000 to 2010.

A BEA analysis for that period – across all classes of businesses, from mining and farming to manufacturing and retail (see Figure 13) – shows that, with more labor productivity, there was no statistically significant decrease in overall employment. At the same time, there was a modest increase in average wages. Meanwhile, the data show that rising labor productivity was associated with a dramatic reduction in the prices of the goods and services produced by that labor; this, of course, was precisely the desired outcome.

Again, though, looking under the hood at the granular details of the overall analysis, one sees the kind of variability inherent with diverse datasets. (See Figure 14.) A variety of specific businesses, such as fabric mills, motor-vehicle parts producers and computer manufacturers, have shown increased labor productivity associated with reductions in employment. That trend was in clear evidence in the automobile industry in the 1960s, when, as noted earlier, President Kennedy launched our modern era's automation anxieties. Cherry-picking and anecdotes don't prove a trend, though. For specific industries, there are other episodic factors that can impact jobs, such as unusual trade or tariff issues, foreign competition, new taxes and regulations targeting a specific business or product.

The pessimists, not to be deterred by evidence showing that job gains are associated with technology's next

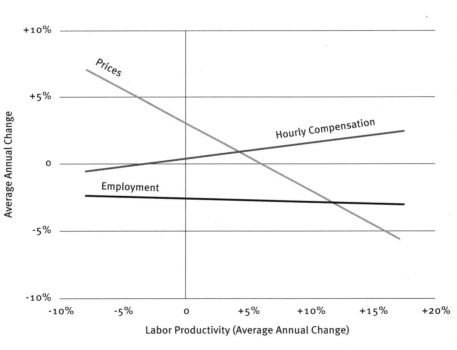

Figure 13 Impact of Productivity on Prices, Wages and Employment, 2000–2010
Source: 2000–2010 BLS Productivity Labor Prices Wages

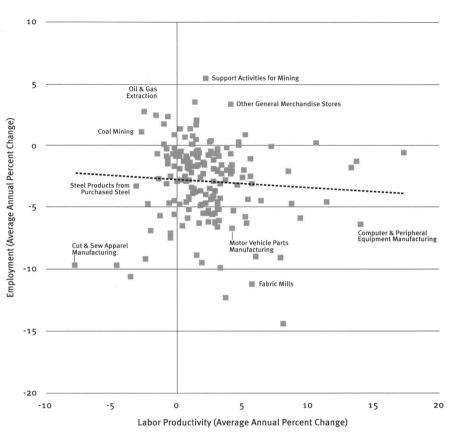

Figure 14 Impact of Productivity on Employment, 2000–2010

The dashed line represents the best-fit relationship between changes in productivity and changes in employment among all industries studied.
Source: US Bureau of Economic Analysis, BLS

59

great leap, redound to another claim: that most of those jobs will be for "knowledge workers" – coders or others with a STEM (science, technology, engineering, math) education. Economist Robert Samuelson diagnosed the emerging tech-centric economy as the "curse of middle-aged capitalism," with "both strong and weak" companies on "two separate tracks," one "youthful," the other "middle-aged." The youthful – synonymous with tech, the logic goes – will employ mainly STEM-educated people.

STEM employment is growing fast, but most jobs won't be STEM ones

The problem with the thesis that most jobs will go to those with a STEM degree is simple: the data don't come close to supporting the proposition. Indeed, non-STEM skills are required for the majority of jobs even in most tech companies and especially in the rest of the economy. There *is* a skills shortage in America, but the vast majority of shortages are found in the non-college skilled trades (from machine operators to welders), in which a half-million openings are left unfilled each year.

Nonetheless, over the last half-century the number of people employed as engineers or scientists in America rose from one million to some eight million. That has led to

Today, we stand at the very beginning of the autonomous-robot era: to compare it to the automobile age, we are in the 1890s, awaiting the first Model T.

a tripling of the share of all occupations for engineers and scientists. But one can get big growth rates by starting from a very small number. STEM jobs still constitute only about 6% of the total workforce. In fact, there are still fewer people writing software than there are currently employed as farmers and agricultural workers.

The other popular thesis in our new information era is that America is facing a deficit of STEM-educated graduates for the tech sector. It is true that there is intense demand for, and a shortage of, people with certain specific degrees useful for data analytics, machine learning and AI. But, overall, America produces each year roughly 50% more STEM graduates than there are STEM job openings for them. More than 11 million Americans today have a STEM degree but are employed in a non-STEM job. As for those specific areas with shortages of suitable graduates (e.g., mathematics), history has shown that students capable of pursuing a STEM education quickly figure out where the money is and serially oversupply each "hot" sector as it emerges.

Of course, educators and employers are eager to have access to people who are familiar with technology, but many of the skills they're seeking don't require a STEM degree. Furthermore, as Google, for one, recently revealed in the results of a comprehensive internal study, a STEM degree was the last of the top eight qualities or skills found to be important for employee advancement. The top seven were all the so-called soft skills, relating to communication and cooperation, as well as the need to be a "critical thinker." As any educator will attest, such skills are not necessarily associated with – and, some argue, are even counter to – what's provided in a STEM curriculum.

We also know from history that engineers strive to make technology not only better and cheaper, but also easier to operate by non-experts. They have achieved particular success in this regard with the software many people use casually today. AI of the future, even coding, will become increasingly easy for laypeople's use too, helping more people become "knowledge workers" while likely collaterally reducing demand for many coders. In fact, if that were not the trajectory, there would be no real prospect for rapid growth.

None of this obviates the fact that society *is* migrating toward an era of ambient computing wherein every business and job will have increasingly knowledge-centric features. But when it comes to STEM skills, some pundits seem to conflate two related but different issues: the role that STEM workers will play in propelling the infrastructure of the new era, and the number and kinds of other jobs that an expanded economy will generate.

Despite what logic and history dictate, the farm-to-factory transition of the last century continues to be the favored analogy for the future. The argument goes that whereas last time, as automation replaced farmers, those who were put out of work were able to find "skilled trades" in an expanding manufacturing sector, this time, as automation eliminates the need for manufacturing skills, there will be nowhere for the displaced to go for work except (the thesis continues) low-paying menial work as an alternative to applying for a UBI and staying home. This argument fails in two core ways.

The idea that the 20th century's expanding industrial society saw manufacturing absorb most of those formerly employed in farming is *prima facie* wrong. While manufacturing expansion absorbed many workers, the service sector has always been bigger than the manufacturing sector (as noted earlier; see Figure 5) and was the major source of employment for those exiting agriculture.

But more to the fundamental flaw here, the core demand for output in each sector is a critical variable when determining where future employment will be found. If labor productivity improves faster than demand for labor's output (of products or services), this arithmetically means fewer overall jobs will be needed to serve that demand. That's what happened to farming: agricultural productivity soared, while food demand grew relatively slowly. But this trajectory of demand for future manufacturing output is profoundly different. Demand for agricultural products has a limited and definable maximum, whereas the demand for manufactures is nearly unlimited.

Global demand for agricultural output is, for obvious reasons, essentially linked to (slow) population growth rates, plus the rise in per-person consumption for those underfed today. Thus we know with remarkable precision maximum future volumes: people in the future won't consume more than about twice what the poorest consume today. China, the most populous country, has largely already made this transition over the past 50 years.

On the other hand, we know that far more than a doubling is possible in the global consumption of manufactured items such as air conditioners, cars, computers, furnishing and luxuries. In many cases, potential demand is 10 to 100 times that of today. Individuals' "appetite" for goods will grow far faster than the world's population or their desire to consume food. With cars, for example, in most industrial countries there are more than 700 vehicles per 1,000 people; that is, more cars than registered drivers. In most of the world's emerging economies, one finds the inverse: several hundred people per single car owned. There is similar potential growth in demand for every other category of existing products and product-dependent services, such as air travel.

On top of that, as inventions continually lead to new products and services, rising wealth leads to the demand for those previously nonexistent things. There was no demand for cars, radios or smartphones until they were invented. Thus, it should be unsurprising that history shows that agricultural output roughly tracks population growth, while industrial output far outpaces both. (See Figure 15.) This pattern of the last half-century in America and other industrial nations will be repeated in the future everywhere else.

Furthermore, demand for goods accelerates as prices drop – precisely the outcome of labor-productivity gains. In short, there is every reason to believe that demand for manufacturing output will continue to grow far faster than demand for agricultural products, rendering moot the factory-follows-farm jobs analogy.

A similar argument could be mounted for healthcare industries, in which demand for both services and products

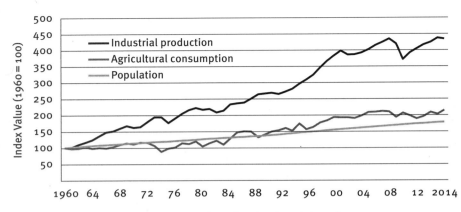

Figure 15 Growth in Consumption of Food and Industrial Products vs. Population in America, 1960–2014
Source: U.S. Department of Agriculture, St. Louis Federal Reserve

is certainly rising faster than population growth rates. Labor-productivity-induced price reductions would accelerate demand and create more jobs there, too.

But while the idea of a wholesale migration from industrial to "knowledge" work is flawed, this does not mean that today's technological transformations will be free of challenging disruptions. The importance and value of the IT-centric infrastructures and the associated jobs are undeniable; they are at the epicenter of today's economic and social transformations. Thus sociologist Daniel Bell was correct in his prediction of the emergence of a new social stratification around tech elites. Negative media coverage is now commonly focused on the behaviors of the tech elites, whom some are labeling "tech's robber barons."

We've seen "this movie" before. Over the nation's history, each technological revolution created great wealth, and great social and political power, for the pioneers and captains of the new enterprises. The railroad age gave us the phrase "robber baron" and the wealthiest citizens in American history thus far. Measured in inflation-adjusted terms, Jeff Bezos and Bill Gates, today's two richest citizens, are now approaching the wealth of Rockefeller and Vanderbilt.

Long booms, and challenging disruptions, follow great infrastructure shifts

All the players of the Cloud age have yet to emerge. Odds are most of the future's dominant ones are still invisible or yet in some entrepreneur's dreams. The rise of the automobile age provides a useful analogy. By 1920, a few decades after "first fission" of the auto age, 10% of the population had a car and hundreds of U.S. automakers had sprung up, creating a lot of early wealth and much popular excitement.

It took time to conquer the complexities of manufacturing reliable, affordable cars and to develop all the associated industries and infrastructures. But once that happened, things really took off. By 1937, the percentage of car ownership was 25%; by 1957, it was 40%; today, it's 85%. Along the way, the entire structure of the American economy was transformed, stimulating growth and new employment across the landscape. Detroit was the Silicon Valley of its day, but the benefits of ubiquitous personal transportation boosted the entire nation.

Today, in equivalent terms to the automobile age's trajectory, when it comes to practical AI and the Cloud, we are likely at 1920, with the inflection point in sight. Meanwhile, when it comes to autonomous robots, we stand circa 1890 awaiting the first Model T.

Every major infrastructure shift in U.S. history propelled the nation to greater prosperity. Every era created more new companies and jobs, most of them entirely unanticipated, than were lost from the less-productive centers of the economy. The central challenge in the transition of our era is *not* the prospect of the end of work and systemic high unemployment. Our challenge is the same as in earlier eras: the moral and political imperative to deal with the inevitable disruptions that occur along the way to enhanced prosperity.

Every great transition has been matched by disruptions to a minority of the population. Those disruptions have often been socially painful, even violent. For examples we don't have to look back as far in history as the famously cited Luddite protests, or the lesser-known Swing riots of 1830s England, when farm laborers displaced by the steam-thresher set fire to hay bales and farms and sabotaged the machines.

The labor strikes and riots of early-20th-century America offer other examples, as do the first modern automation anxieties, in particular those noted earlier from the Kennedy era. Every time big changes came along, it was

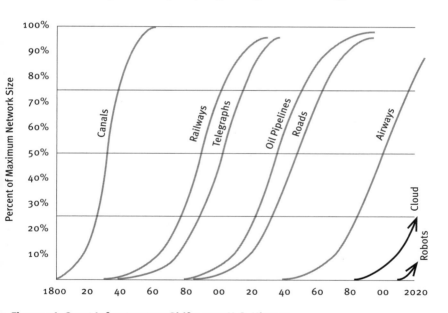

Figure 16 Great Infrastructure Shifts over U.S. History:
Time from Inception to Fully Built Infrastructure
Source: Adapted from Grübler and Nakicenovic, Long Waves, Technology Diffusion, and Substitution *(1991)*

difficult to imagine where and how most people in the future would be employed, but it seemed obvious who would be losing out in the transition.

The hallmark of the 20th century, compared to earlier eras, was the emergence of government programs to help those disrupted by automation and attendant progress that otherwise benefited the majority of citizens. We already see the same old proposals being offered again by politicians, pundits and tech titans for our time. In fact, every proposal suggested, whether reeducation, retrain-

Few economists realize that the opportunity to ameliorate the coming employment disruptions lies in the very tools that are about to cause them.

ing or a Universal Basic Income, is identical to those offered a half-century ago.

Although those traditional solutions still have a role to play, there is precious little innovation being offered either in the specific proposals or in how to implement them to deal with our emerging employment disruptions. Few economists realize that the opportunity to ameliorate the disruptions lies in the very tools that are about to cause them.

Unlike early hardware-centric productivity revolutions, the new software-centric and data-rich infrastructure allows us a unique opportunity to identify who will be disrupted, when and how. The information infrastructure offers ways of imagining far more efficient and effective means of providing solutions, from matching skills with employers to providing remote and low-cost online and even "virtual" means of up-skilling. In effect, bringing greater efficiency and productivity to *those* services is now possible with AI and automation.

To further cement a more enlightened transition in this new era, rather than have governments lead an effort to address employment disruption by using "tech," the tech industries themselves should lead that effort. The leading tech companies should organize a collective program to pioneer innovative solutions anchored in the new infrastructure. Such programs, of course, entail a cost to businesses. But such costs, if self-imposed, would likely be lower than anything that politicians and bureaucrats would eventually come up with. And who would doubt that Silicon Valley could be far more innovative than Capitol Hill in crafting tech-driven solutions?

Harvard Business professor Michael Toffel suggests that, since the 1990s, there has been something of an overall cultural shift in the private sector. We see an increasing focus on what happens outside an individual business – in particular, in the supply chain associated with a business –

and the unintended impacts of internal business activities.

Forbes magazine recently surveyed 72,000 Americans to identify which firms people thought were "just"; that is, which companies were "producing quality goods, treating customers well, minimizing environmental impact, supporting the communities businesses operate in, committing to ethical (and diverse) leadership, and above all, treating workers well." Tech firms accounted for 39 of the top 100.

Perhaps Michael Toffel is right, and we live in a time of great cultural shift, not just a technological one. We shall yet see how today's tech leaders choose to manage the employment and social fallout they are beginning to cause to the minority as they acquire greater wealth for themselves and their employees. Transitions of this scale are inherently challenging and disruptive. But in the end there will be more, not less, work in the age of robots.

First American edition published in 2018 by Encounter Books, an activity of Encounter for Culture and Education, Inc., a nonprofit, tax exempt corporation. Encounter Books website address: www.encounterbooks.com

Manufactured in the United States and printed on acid-free paper. The paper used in this publication meets the minimum requirements of ANSI/NISO Z39.48–1992 (R 1997) (*Permanence of Paper*).

FIRST AMERICAN EDITION

LIBRARY OF CONGRESS CATALOGING-IN-PUBLICATION DATA

Names Names: Mills, Mark P., author.
Title: Work in the age of robots / by Mark P. Mills.
Description: New York : Encounter Books, [2018] |
Series: Encounter intelligence ; 4
Identifiers: LCCN 2018013646 (print) | LCCN 2018014723 (ebook) |
ISBN 9781641770286 (ebook) | ISBN 9781641770279 (pbk. : alk. paper)
Subjects: LCSH: Automation—Economic aspects—United States. |
Robotics—Economic aspects—United States. | Labor market—
United States. | Labor productivity—United States.
Classification: LCC HC110.A9 (ebook) | LCC HC110.A9 M55 2018 (print) |
DDC 331.25—dc23
LC record available at https://lccn.loc.gov/2018013646

10 9 8 7 6 5 4 3 2 1